Bilingual Press/Editorial Bilingüe
Canto Cosas

Series Editor
Francisco Aragón

Publisher
Gary D. Keller

Executive Editor
Karen S. Van Hooft

Associate Editors
Adriana M. Brady
Brian Ellis Cassity
Amy K. Phillips
Linda K. St. George

Address
Bilingual Press
Hispanic Research Center
Arizona State University
PO Box 875303
Tempe, Arizona 85287-5303
(480) 965-3867

boomerang

POEMS BY
Brenda Cárdenas

Bilingual Press/Editorial Bilingüe
Tempe, Arizona

Library of Congress Cataloging-in-Publication Data

Cárdenas, Brenda
    Boomerang / Brenda Cárdenas.
        p. cm.
    Poems using both English and Spanish; some are entirely in one language, others include both languages in the same poem (codeswitching).
    ISBN 978-1-931010-53-5 (pbk. : alk. paper)
    I. Title.

    PS3603.A7345B66 2008
    811'.6—dc22

                                                            2008024706

PRINTED IN THE UNITED STATES OF AMERICA

Front cover art: Micro World 3 *(2007) by Miguel Cortez*
Cover and interior design by Bill Greaves, Concept West

This publication is supported in part by an award from the National Endowment for the Arts.

NATIONAL
ENDOWMENT
FOR THE ARTS

Source acknowledgments are on p. xi.

Canto Cosas

Funded in part by grants from the National Endowment for the Arts and the Arizona Commission on the Arts, this new series is designed to give further exposure to Latina and Latino poets who have achieved a significant level of critical recognition through individual chapbooks and publication in periodicals or anthologies or both, but who have not necessarily had their own books of poetry published. Under the watchful eye of series editor, poet, and small press publisher Francisco Aragón, the books in Canto Cosas aim to reflect the aesthetic diversity in American poetry. There are no restrictions on ethnicity, nationality, philosophy, ideology, or language; we will simply continue our commitment to producing high-quality poetry. The books in this series will also feature introductions by more established voices in the field.

*For all my friends and family
with your keys, your prayers, your recipes,
your open arms and hearts,
with your lights always on*

boomerang

Contents

III

IV

Acknowledgments

Many thanks to the editors of the following anthologies and literary journals in which some of the poems in this book (or different versions of them) first appeared:

Achiote Seeds: "Diffraction," "La cuentista," "Someone"

After Hours: A Journal of Chicago Writing and Art: "Empty Spaces," "Turning"

Between the Heart and the Land / Entre el corazón y la tierra: Latina Poets in the Midwest (MARCH/Abrazo Press, 2001): "Report from the Temple of Confessions in Old Chicano English," "Sound Waves: Intensidad—Ñ," "Sound Waves: Duración—V," "Through Arms and Hands"

The Book of Voices, <www.e-poets.net>: "When We Moved Away from Tía Elia's and Uncle Karel's, 1968"

The City Visible: Chicago Poetry for the New Century (Cracked Slab Books, 2007): "If"

The Heartlands Today: Community (The Firelands Writing Center, 1994): "Feast"

Learning by Heart: Contemporary American Poetry about School (University of Iowa Press, 1999): "Lecciones de lengua"

Poetic Voices Without Borders (Gival Press, 2005): "Al Mestizaje," "Cartoon Coyote Goes Po-Mo," "Poema para los tin-tun-teros/Poem for the Tin-tun-teros," "The History Beneath Our Skin," "Zacuanpapalotls"

Prairie Schooner: "Abuelo y sus cuentos: Origin of the Bird-Beak Mole," "Sound Waves: Tono—D"

RATTLE: Poetry for the 21st Century: "Hay una mujer/There Is a Woman," "Sonnet for Thunder Lovers and Primary Colors"

Tamaqua: "Centripetal Motion"

Under the Pomegranate Tree: The Best New Latino Erotica (Washington Square Press, Pocket Books: 1996): "Our Language"

Wicked Alice Poetry Journal: "Medicine," "Me and My Cuz"

The Wind Shifts: New Latino Poetry (University of Arizona Press, 2007): "Song"

Some poems also appeared in the chapbook *From the Tongues of Brick and Stone* (Momotombo Press, 2005).

The lyric quoted in "Blues Mama" is from "The Good Life" by S. Distel and J. Reardon, Intersong Music, ASCAP.

To Gary Keller, Karen Van Hooft, and all at Bilingual Review Press, my deepest respect and appreciation.

To Frances Aparicio, Renée Cárdenas, Eleazar Delgado, Juan Felipe Herrera, Janet Jennerjohn, Maurice Kilwein Guevara, María Meléndez, Maricarmen Moreno, Milton Rodríguez, Jeanne Theoharris, Richard Tillinghast, and Johanny Vázquez Paz: For your encouragement, guidance, and many kindnesses, I offer the grandest pachanga of gratitude my heart could ever conjure. And to Francisco Aragón, guest of honor, I send an entire mariachi band and the mother of all gritos.

To my parents, Diane and José Cárdenas, my aunt Elia and uncle Karel, and my partner, Roberto Harrison: For you, never enough thanks; because of you, always enough love.

Boomerang Light

Juan Felipe Herrera

The beginning is empty; however, the emptiness is plural—there are limitless space quadrants in the vast, open, uncharted field of "lost sounds." And it is here in the nameless and formless universe where *she* rises, "braying the silence away." What brays? you may ask. Listen: a woman half-panther, a storyteller with a snout and "coyote moonshine," with "belly to earth." The first pages of this multivoiced collection point to the various elements, figures, and vibratory word scales of Cárdenas's "boomerang."

This curved, V-like flying figure is the woman-body in motion for-itself and for-others. Self-determined and self-propelled, it can take the shape, vocality, velocity, and temperatures it desires—across time, herstory, and space. And it can also ingest, incubate, pulse, and migrate internally and beyond the parameters of its form. After it has consumed the universe, the boomerang—one-half made of explosion, the other of pronouncement—"leaves a rhythm scattered on the wind."

This collection is volatile the way a panther or trickster coyote is capable of deft performance at night or at dawn when all is quiet and seems to be in order. As the boomerang rings and rattles across loves, deaths, stories, language(s), growled and lettered utterances, rhythm narratives, and lives it leaps across the last four decades. It demarcates a new era in Chicana and Latina poetics in the Américas.

The text here gathers much from the last forty years of Chicana poetry pioneers who dared to speak of woman blood, woman body, woman familia, woman talk, and woman mind. Here, key pioneers are Yolanda Luera, Alma Villanueva, Lorna Dee Cervantes, Evangelina Vigil, Bernice Zamora, Margarita Robles, and Gloria Anzaldúa.

Perhaps like the new twenty-first century generation of Chicana and Latina poets, such as Gabriela Jáuregui, Carmen Giménez-Smith, and Amalia Álvarez, Cárdenas's radical contributions have more to do with multivocal velocity, a fiery heteroglossia—that is, the rapid shifts of different ways of woman-speaking *and* cultural hybridity, the fusions of various cultural sounds, stanzaic rhythms, and ways of being—than with a homogenous feminism as elaborated within previous texts. Indeed, the Américas are a boomerang-shaped hemisphere.

For Cárdenas, the new poetics is one of exploded boundaries in simultaneous motion going outward, then inward. All at once, *Boomerang* can easily be seen as a bestiary, a children's alphabet book, an Afro-Caribbean percussion tablet, and the shaman's shape-shifting "spinning stone" of the self *and selves.*

In a matter of moments we move across time, space, gender, and species:

> Perhaps the cuentista
> is half panther /
> half man—
> green by day /
> black by night. ("El cuentista")

We open the book of letters for the new speaker:

> This is the *V* in Cabeza de Vaca
> sweating the salt of the bay
> in a migration that halts and hovers. ("Duración—*V*")

The text is an Afro-Caribbean beat, a score of contrapuntal eulogy and conjure:

> Este para los timbaleros, los bateristas, los tin-tun-teros,
> los que tocan con cucharas en sus estufas
> con lápices en sus escritorios
> con uñas y nudillos en mesas, muebles, sus propias cabezas
> con puños contra paredes

y dedos en las espinas y curvas de sus amantes, danzantes.

("Poema para los tin-tun-teros")

Percussive bops and ratchets implode into and out of the text;
they slap each other, pour, and blister:

Erre, te quiero erre,

por mi barrio encarrujando

en tu carro zurrido

donde me estás arrebatando,

mi amante garrido. ("Timbre—*RR*")

Only a shamanic speaker, it seems, is capable of such expert
boomerang-shaped sweeps over the image, text, and story-body.
What emerges?

We are—

one life passing through the prism

of all others, gathering color and song,

cempazuchil and drum

to leave a rhythm scattered on the wind,

dust tinting the tips of fingers

as we slip into our new light. ("Zacaunpapalotls")

"The beginning is empty," Cárdenas writes in the first poem in
this collection. Emptiness is a boomerang of sorts. From the void it
shoots out in a wild, reckless spin, defying the all-knowing circle,
challenging the ancient ellipse. Yet, it leaves us an opening, an
unsung note in the air for all things to emerge into their fullness.
It is interconnected with the past and the present—voices, sounds,
places, rhythms, bodies in their journey toward the future-body.
Here is that future-form coming straight back at you.

Suddenly, as rare things will, it vanished.

—Elizabeth Barrett Browning

Empty Spaces

She is a switchblade afraid of the hint in a two-second glint that
might spring you an arm's length away. *I fear.* She kisses close, to
shut the open gate of hunger, heavy-footed as history perched on
her chest. *Empty spaces.* She never rests. Stumbling through the
clutter of language, she rummages cramped closets for her lost
sounds—i griegas y erres—tumbling like marbles spilled in the
attic. *Spaces I fear.* She mainlines white noise—a guest persistent
as rain flooding her muted room. *Spaces.* She adds another hue to
the walls crawling with orange and blue that zigzag the curves of
her world to the ceiling. *I fear empty spaces.* She is reeling in a
ravenous subjunctive that would doubt its own bones were it not
for her grip slipping from your moist shoulders to the winter of
metal bedposts. *Spaces I empty.* She grinds against you, minding
only the bland blue sky that filters through the O'Keefe hollow
of her pelvis. *I empty fear.* In this abyss, she comes, braying the
silence away.

If

(for Roberto)

Cobalt dusk
Icicles break free
                    from our collarbones,
                              ribs,
                                        pelvic branches,
perfect pearls of light.

Bathe me
          in freshwater eyes. When the doubt
in the *if* that is this

                    noun
                         floods your alone,

               sit in the radiator's steam and hiss,
                    allow it to give you your breath.

               Then pour it
                         out the window.

               Melt my snow,
so I don't have to shovel *ifs*.   No turn
                    in the woods is wrong
                         when you follow
                                   the tracks of something
                         that follows you,

               links end to beginning. Infinity.

               Half empty, half empathy,
                    if is a tender conjunction.

4

You tell me to trust the unfinished clauses
              spilling from the highest branches
                    into my lap.
They are not patterns; they are snowflakes.
They are not feathers; they are flight.

          I tell you to trust the unfinished nest
              they fall from
              in the spring that has not yet arrived.

          There is nothing arbitrary about it—

          that circle of twigs and litter,
          rinds, hair and clover
              kissed like some ancient shrine
                    by the sun.

El cuentista

(after a linoleum print by René Arceo)

I
The storyteller sits cross-legged on a cane stool,
coyote's moonshine in his eyes. He pens tales
on amate sheaves, each word a whisker
sprouting from his snout. As phrases appear,
one foot twitches, stirring the quiet air.
The other, planted firmly on the floor, opens
like a trumpet flower to birth a child.
Belly to earth, the hatchling crawls on forearms
past the ovary of his father's ankle, out the toes.

Once free, his legs will grow long as legends.
His father will look him in the eye, wave
goodbye, yellow into memory. But in the oval
window of the young one's ear, something will stir,
bristle his fur as it squirms along aqueducts,
the open folds of cords. It will stretch
its neck in the cloud of his breath
and howl at stars gathering in a distant field
to share their news of the ancestors.

II
Perhaps the cuentista
            is half panther /
            half man—
                        green by day /
                        black by night.

As he paints glyphs
onto paper bound
by spit and ash
they rise and dart
like ferrets
under his chair
afraid of who might emerge
next
from the birth canals
of his feet.   A robot
powers forward
on tank tracks churning   from the left ankle.
A bullyboy claws
his way out
of the right
only to grow
into a girl
so cancan leggy
her polka dot dress shrinks
to a midriff.
Cave woman feet
muscled as myth
could crush
in one soft step
the Lilliputian she used to be.

Yet even she waves
so long
when the beast breathes
a mare
that rears on hind legs
and whinnies
at the yellow stars—

What news of the ancestors?

7

III
What do we compose with our hands
that we have not conceived with our feet?

See with our eyes
that we have not imagined with our breath?

What news is not memory?
What memory not news?

Calculations

"I don't know what to tell you.
Your daughter doesn't understand
math. Numbers trouble her, leave
her stuck on ground zero."

> *Y fueron los mayas*
> *quienes imaginaron el cero,*
> *un signo para nada, para todo,*
> *en sus gran calculaciones.*

> Is zero the velvet swoop into dream,
> the loop into plumes of our breath?

"I suggest you encourage languages.
Already she knows a little Spanish,
and *you* can teach her more of that.
She lives for story time."

> In the beginning there was nothing.
> Then the green of quetzal wings.

> *Las historias siguen cambiando,*
> *sus verdades vigorizadas*
> *con cada narración*
> *como $X \times X = X^2$*

Abuelo y sus cuentos:
Origin of the Bird-Beak Mole

Abuelito, what's that on your arm?

       ¿Este? This little bump?

Sí, ¿qué es?

       Pues, oye, un día cuando era joven
       estaba trabajando en un jardín bellísimo
       cuando lo and behold a little bird
       swooped down and stuck his,
       how do you say?

His beak.

       Sí, his beak in my arm,
       and I twisted and I twisted
       en círculos, around and around,
       until his beak broke off
       right in my muscle. Y ya, mira,
       tengo su nariz en el brazo.

But abuelito, what happened to the bird?

              Pues, está en México.

In México?

       Sí, niña, the bird stayed
       en las montañas con sus amigos
       jactándose de su herida de combate.

But grandpa, how can he talk?
How will he even live without a beak?

Oh, you know, you lose a little here,
a little there. He will learn.

Cornflowers

She says my hair smells
like corn tortillas.
I raise an eyebrow.
After all those honeysuckle
and papaya shampoos,
I can't believe my scalp
hasn't soaked up
the scent of blossom
or the perfume of rainfall.
No, she's my mother,
and she insists
that even as a little girl,
my whole bedroom breathed
corn tortillas.

Pressing nose to pillowcase,
I search for masa,
reach back before
molcajete and plow
to a dusky meadow,
its bed of soil flecked
with teosinte,
ancestor grasses.

Up through the dark
follicles of my skull
covered in sun-cracked husks,
push the black-brown silk strands,
cocooning thirsty kernels.
Maíz sprouts into fields of thought
bearing hybrid rows of words
that fall like teeth
from the mouths of the dead.

12

Carne y hueso / Flesh and Bone

Brothers don't fight! he warns
through clenched teeth as he drags
his sons to the kitchen pantry, orders
them to strip off their sweaty T-shirts,
and salts their naked backs. *Lámenlo*,
he tells them, lick the grains off
each other's skin. He watches, arms
folded across his chest, as they take
turns until their throats sting
and their thick tongues have brushed
each other's sticky espaldas clean.

He never mentions his own brothers:
How Emerio sank to the blood-
spattered planks of a cantina,
bullets pumping into his chest
like the drills he'd driven into
Veracruz oil fields for pesos,
while thick pools bubbled
around the knee-high boots of the rich.

How Jesús fell in la plaza,
head smashed against a fountain
as he sipped its arc of water,
a neighbor's envious knife
wedged between a woman's kisses,
one on each shoulder blade.

Or how Julio, the only living
brother, fled Mazamitla's fields
for Milwaukee's tanneries.
How in the late hours of a double

shift, he slid into a chemical spill,
acids gnawing at flesh, fusing
the St. Christopher medal
around his neck to collarbone.

¡No se pelean los hermanos!
this father insists,
those he lost
stung back to life
through the pores
on his sons' curved spines.

Turning

At least 300 people have been killed in the
rugged southern state of Chiapas, since clashes
began four years ago between Indian guerrillas
[Zapatistas] fighting for greater rights and armed
militia members opposed to their cause.
—Ian Fisher, the *New York Times*,
December 26, 1997

Another year turns south of the Loop,
marches beneath el arco de La Villita,
"Circle the sidewalk!" bark Chicago's blue-
fisted, "Keep moving!" billy clubs in tow.
I weave my ribboned voice into the chant,
    Zapata vive, vive
wrap my fingers around the stick stapled
to a black Zapatista mask kerchiefed in red
    La lucha sigue, sigue
that Teo passes me in this dizzying tread
over the same ground.
Presidente Zedillo's papier-mâché head bobs
above prison stripes, as he sprints up
and down Calle Veintiséis, spins
beneath the blows of cardboard machetes
that slice and scoop the air like scavengers.
Some laugh at this spectacle, then shout
    ¡Alto a la militarización!
at this theater of the absurd.
    ¡Alto a la represión!
Our circle stretches to an oval,
January breaths rising in chorus.

I think of the friends who turned
at midnight to hold me
in the hoops of their arms,
as the Earth completed its revolution.
I think of my uncle's cancer
nesting in his hunger,
in the snipped and sheared sack
that remained after the war,
after ulcers had shredded almost all
of his stomach. And I think of you,
camarada, in the jungles of Chiapas,
waiting like a cat for night to shield you
from the eyes of federales, armies
who blockaded the villages, camps—
Maya refugee cells of starvation;

waiting
so you could sneak past barricades
to bear witness, bring food,
place your body between los tzotziles
and the death squads that would turn
just before the year and open fire
on the people of Acteal.
The army would not let you pass,
so you waited ten miles
from the sunlit massacre.

Our oval slows to a rectangle.
And who of us now is not thinking
of los tzotziles embracing 45 caskets—
1 infant, 14 children, 21 women, 9 men—
while their murderers wove
between the mourners
in a chain link of intimidation?

From La Villita in Chicago
we can shout, pray, pledge,
but when bullhorns rest
and the streets clear, we turn
back to frosted windshields,
rumble of the 'L', a stop
at the panadería where we pile
our tray high with pan dulce.
The lumps of dough and sugar
catch in my throat. And I think

of doctors slicing my uncle's stomach
from his body like a rotten wedge of fruit
one week after babies were carved
from their mothers' bellies at Acteal—
how they will never savor nor crave,
and he will eat for the rest of his life,
four bites at a time, all day long
to keep himself from starving.

I think of you now, camarada,
only hours away from me,
alone in your room, tarps pulled tight
over the windows to seal out
any crease of light, the fire so low
in the stove that you can watch
your own breath dissipate
into the kerosene shadows.
You do not call on me to bring blankets
or tea; to listen to the ten-year list
of bodies you identified
in the morgues of Guatemala
after walking with them to the store,
the river, the milpas where masa begins.

You do not ask me to repeat the 45 names
on crosses piercing the Tzotzil soil.
You do not call,
further from me now
than that plot of earth where their corpses lie,
than the hope
that I force myself to swallow.

Someone

(after a photograph in the George W. Brown, Jr., Ojibwe Museum
and Cultural Center, Lac du Flambeau Reservation, Wisconsin)

I
Someone Traveling
Sound Of Eating
High In The Sky

Traveling Sound
Of The High Sky
In Someone Eating

Eating The Sound
In Sky Travel
Of Someone High

Traveling In The Sky
Eating Someone
Of High Sound

Some Sound
In The Sky Eating
One Traveling High

Sounding Sky High
Eating Of The One
In Some Travel

In Sound Sky
Of Some High One Eating
Traveling

Sounding High Of Travel
So me Eating
In The One Sky

Someone Traveling
Sound Of Eating
High In The Sky

Someone

II
Between Someone Traveling
and young High In The Sky
stands Sound Of Eating

Leader, he
provides for

Someone

III
Someone Traveling
knows the camera
aims to capture
one tribe

draw you closer
to note similar details
in the regalia—
canoe shape
of their moccasins
order of
bead bead bead bead
bone bead bead

claw bead bead bone
bead bead bead bead
tooth

Knows you will see
the same stare
from the same eyes
that feel the same way
about you

IV
I have no idea
what Someone Traveling knows
or doesn't know
no idea
which maps he carries
in his mind his heart his pocket

V
For all we know
there is no bond—
not in the journey
not in the meal
not even
under the sky

Different ages heights
different ranks tastes moods eyes
different cheekbones
For all we know
these are three
separate

someones

VI
If this were not 1895 but 1965
the camera an Instant Polaroid
perhaps High In The Sky
would tie their portrait
to a helium balloon
and send all three of them
to the clouds
where they would bleed
together
into the moist, white puffs
and spill
like iridescent gills
of rainbow trout
or like muddied waters
sprayed about by the wind

or like a people

or like someone traveling

VII

The photographer	like the poet
has no musket	no glass beads
no spices	no pelts
no game	no land
no fishing rights	no canoe
no new motorboat	no full bingo card
no casino	no first treaty torn and taped
no gasoline	no reservation
nothing	to trade
in upturned hands.	

For this
High In The Sky
doesn't give a damn
For this
he will give the camera
his most defiant, most blissful
smile   For this
he will give the camera
his best shot

VIII
Sound of laughter—
someone deep
inside the earth
poking fun
at the black box
about to devour
someone's spirit

Can you hear
the high sounds
of your own eating?

IX
I mean
Someone Traveling
Sound Of Eating
High In The Sky
These are translations
                traveling
of their names
                eating

on a paper
        sky

These are their names

X
Someone Traveling
Sound Of Eating
High In The Sky

At Aldebaran

Bringing in the new year
    coon paw and deer hoof
imprinted in last year's snow
        on the west ridge, melting.

Jumble of bloody feathers
    striped brown and white
        mark the icy path's
        daily encounters.
   Silent until shudders
        heavy as canvas flapping
        in a squall, a Chinese kite—
          the flight of wild turkey
wing.

      Blue jay dives
      an Indigo splash
        and cardinal beams
        berry red in the thick fog.
          Chickadee acrobatics
           above steep slopes
          tease the air we breathe.

Bringing in the new year—
    fur carpet crescents
the rib cage,
picked clean by crow,
    of nearly devoured doe—
        severed hind legs lying
        perpendicular to the body
          head resting in a skirmish of snow.
    Hollow sockets stare black.

We see with the eyes she has lost,
   become the hills we are climbing.
      Pause
                  quietly move on.

I imagine that yes is the only living thing.

—e.e. cummings

Medicine

(after a print by Jeff Abbey Maldonado)

Lacandona, the rain forest,
is a woman draped in solitude,

her hair a translucent cocoon.
In her lungs, a clearing

where stone pillars
hold arches of sky.

As tangled roots
fill her tilted womb,

she turns her back on waiting.
Her dark shoulder passes

through temple walls
to the internal refuge

where she shapes masks
of creatures she imagines

spawning from her,
hatching from the splintered

shells of eggs
too thin to incubate.

There is a man under the tent
of her eyebrow,

an old ghost
in the slit of her stare,

There is a rustling
beneath her skin.

Axolotl, the salamander, slips
like green corn into her mouth,

clicks his toenails
against her teeth,

nestles in the harvest
under her tongue,

twists down
the stalk of her spine.

She searches for his tails
lost in her limbs,

caught on the branches of her ribs,
medicine to clear

the red clouds from her eyes,
draw the poison

from her punctured flesh
before it swims

into the seventh generation.
Sometimes, dusk soothes

her slashed back, cools its burns,
peels away the day's pain.

And if we turn
in the evening mist,

we can hear her
whisper our names.

Our Language

When I sigh
I am breathing you
back out of me.
Like smoke you pause,
then melt into air,
the silent *e* of love
or *hache* of hábito.

Háblame, you say,
yet my next breath
draws you in with the air
hissing past teeth
because I do not know
where I want you
or what awkward syntax
I'll leave twisted
in the whispering sheets.

The hush of your hands
reaches me from every shadow.
You kiss the slats of skin open
to the striped dawn
of the window blind.
You kiss these warm *l's*
of light and depart.

In the caesura between hours and days,
weeks, I stroke watercolors.
The blue sinks deep
as the resonant pitch
of your vocal chords,
an anaphora of waves
lapping to the shore

until the paper is satiated.
I am not.

We work in English,
make love in Spanish
and code-switch past our indecision.
On days filled with your absence,
I think in sinalefas
and trace you in the ring left
by my morning coffee cup.
If only I could touch
the amber circles of your eyes,
kiss your liquid pupils
when they dilate, enticed.
Then I'd be inside of you
as you so easily
fall into me.

I'd feel the constriction
of an *x* we cannot name,
the multilingual moan of *o's,*
tense Spanish vowels
awaiting release.
Then the loose
twirling of an *erre*
down our spines,
down the soft sides of our arms,
líquidas vibrantes
of our blood.
This is how I want you—
at once within
and without
like a breath,
a sigh,
a language.

Sound Waves

The river on the other side
of English is carrying the message.
—Víctor Hernández Cruz

Tono—*D*

Some days cushion the dental edges
of our lives like night's cool curve
swerving into the music of light
dándonos the soft shoulder de voz.

Danilo y Diana sweep the street
of its blossoms, dejan piles
of magenta petals lining the gutters
de la colonia. Sí, hay basura,
un cigarillo acá, una lata allá,
but we are blinded by hyacinth
suns bursting from the pavement.

When dusk sinks into la plaza
desliando our braided days,
one hundred black wings
sing in the ceiling of leaves
above Gabo's favorite café,
the curl of *carru carru carru*
floating like a feather to his chair.

This day es una danza de dedos
pressing half moons into clay,
the consonant touch of tongue
to teeth arching the sound away.

Duración—*V*

> *Aquí vuelan aves arracimadas como uvas*

Clusters perch over
open-mouthed stones,
the sculpted men arcing back,
necks straining toward gods and vines,
elbows raised in angles.
Birds veil the starved sun.

> *Aquí vuelan aves arracimadas*

This is the *V* in Cabeza de Vaca
sweating the salt of the bay
in a migration that halts and hovers.
Is it the glint of obsidian that lures
vultures to the eye of earth?
Or jade of stone beasts that pull
thieves up the open-legged vertices
of our pyramids? We vanish

> *Aquí vuelan aves*

in the wind-worn skull of the long-
horn, in mutations making bowls
of eye sockets, cups of its keratin.
We carve hilts for our bowies
from the open jaw. We feed.
Muscle is a buzzard's feast,
our brazos his power to swarm.

> *Aquí*

The new sounds echo.
Our *v's* fling their arms open
and come back to us. *Bs.*

We have seen balas
faster than veins of light
etching the night sky.

They fill our heads with ringing.

Intensidad—Ñ

El campesino rolls
his shoulder blades as he turns
from the furrows toward
the road's curve home,
Otro año, otro día, otra estación;
él ha añejado con su añojal.

~Ñ, the yawn in mañana~

La araña weaves her web of music,
tuning its strings while she sings
de sus compañeras obrando
en las cabañas, labrando
en los campos de caña.
She holds the high notes,
pulling filaments taut.
And when a fly's wing
touches one fiber,
everything vibrates.

~la añagaza del balance~

A cat's arch and curled spine
stretches into the long afternoon.
Sueña con alimañas
espiando de las montañas;
sueña con carne,
the wiry tension
of spring and pounce
on the small-boned
and the broken-winged.

~the sneer of engaño~

Deep heat of day rises
like a serpent from its cool tomb
entrañado beneath the sand,
leaves its tilde trace, la señal,
that loosens and fades,
one moment sliding
into centuries of terrain.

~el diseño antiguo del futuro~

Diamond-skinned Kukulkan,
guiñando desde el cielo,
slides past clouds over the edge
of sun at the tip of Chichén
onto a shadow of stone,
the equinox of a plumed past.

~the slow and brilliant tilt de los añosos~

Coiled in mantillas pañosas
y los llantos oscuros de añoranza,
the fire-eater waits for night
to define the sharp outlines
of his sustenance—la flama
debajo de su ceño
como una piñata abriendo
en una cascada de luz,
su señorada callando los gañidos
desesperados de niños—
eyes squeezed tight
above the blackened rim
of his open mouth.

~Ñ, the grimace of resistance,
un puño contra la saña del hambre~

Timbre—*RR*

Erre, te quiero erre,
por mi barrio encarrujando
en tu carro zurrido
donde me estás arrebatando,
mi amante garrido.
Hay que tener cuidado
cuando estoy a tu lado
porque tu manera escurridiza
me hace mujer arrobadiza.

Sí tú, te hablo a ti
mi río cerrero,
a veces guerrero,
borracho gamberro,
cuervo negro y marrullero
o solamente gorrión,
pajarito en la porrina
de mi doble corazón
volando con voz terrina.

Sí tú, hablo de ti.
Cuando te arrimas a mí
tu canción crece en mis cuerdas vocales.
Cuando me tocas, siento timbales,
maracas y guitarra.
Tienes el único beso
que me para y agarra
de atrás al centro del hueso.

Eres la llegada de un chaparrón
irrumpiendo en mi techo
o los susurros de una sombra marrón

soterrado en mi pecho.
Grito de retumbo y suspiro de aljaba,
terremoto y rurrupata,
la intensidad de una balada,
contigo, nada me hace falta.

Y tú con tus arremuecos errantes
de arriba abajo como torrentes
sus vibraciones abren mis brazos,
mis labios, el temblor de mis besos.
Son como los carros en una carrera
con figuras de ocho en las sierras
y socarrenas de mi tierra,

Por eso, te arrodillo y ofrezco
el azúcar pulposo de mangos
y como el siseo de un refresco
me haces cosquillas con ringorrangos—
con ringorrangos desaferrándome,
sus curvas desencerrándome,
espirales desarropándome,
remolinos desarrollándome

hasta que arribamos en este corrido
de un lío amoroso de voz y sonido
tan tórrido, cariñoso que me has capturado
y en tu armonía, me has arrebujado.
Sí tú, te hablo a ti
erre, que te quiero, erre.

Sonnet for Thunder Lovers and Primary Colors

(When Sweet Nothings Just Don't Cut It)

You're more than soda fizz, than sparklers lit
for kids at play, than fireflies' flit in sky.
You spin around my heart and up my thigh
with the whistle and boom of a bottle rocket.
Baby, those other jugglers' gigolo tricks—
magician's spell and mime's unspoken sigh—
don't turn my head, don't catch my ear or eye,
but *your* mercury rolls in my hip pocket.

Some women like the subtle hints, require
a pastel touch, a whispered cry and blush,
but not me; I am all hyperbole.
Your howls of red, your strokes of green sapphire,
your cayenne kiss, serrano pepper rush
from lip to nape of knee will do for me.

Poema para los tin-tun-teros

Este para los timbaleros, los bateristas, los tin-tun-teros,
los que tocan con cucharas en sus estufas
con lápices en sus escritorios
con uñas y nudillos en mesas, muebles, sus propias cabezas
con puños contra paredes
y dedos en las espinas y curvas de sus amantes, danzantes.

Este para los congueros, los tamboristas, los bongoseros,
los que nunca descansan
con sus tacones siempre golpeando la piel del piso,
zapateando en sus sueños llenos de maracas, güiros y claves,
estos bailadores con pasos tan suaves
y caderas que se mueven como sus *high hats* y tarolas.

Este para los timbaleros, los bateristas, los tin-tun-teros.
Son chingones con sus tormentas de platillos,
sus juegos de palillos que vuelan como alas. Qué malas
sus trampas que no nos permiten trabajar ni dormir,
solamente bailar y cantar, cantar y bailar
y a veces mover la tierra un poquito.

Poem for the Tin-tun-teros

This for the timbaleros, percussionists, tin-tun-teros,
those who tap with spoons on their stoves
with pencils on their desks
with nails and knuckles on tables, beds, their own heads
with fists against walls
and fingers on the spines and curves of their lovers, dancers.

This for the congueros, drummers, bongoseros,
those who never rest
with their staccato heels always hammering the skin of the floor
stomping in their dreams filled with maracas, güiros and claves,
these dancers with steps so smooth
and hips that move like their high hats and snares.

This for the timbaleros, percussionists, tin-tun-teros.
They are bad asses with their cymbal storms
their games of sticks that fly like wings. How scampish
their tricks that won't let us work or sleep
only dance and sing, sing and dance
and sometimes move the earth a little.

Report from the Temple of Confessions in Old Chicano English

(after an installation by Guillermo Gómez-Peña and Roberto
Sifuentes)

Se cruzan canyons   en el templo de confessions.
Language lies   across the barbed lines,
piles of its limbs   pierced y pinchados.
Risky recordings   reveal what we think
of the Other   offering his objectified body
to the river rats   who ride his wet back,
the coro de coyotes   who crave his flesh,
the wheyfaced who   whisper their sin in his ear,
the translators who trap   and trade his tongue,
la raza who receive him,   la raza who repel him.

In this chamber the chill   of chicken flesh—
pollito mojado   picoso y picado,
the black body   bag of the repatriated.
Here the distorted words   of debutantes y do-gooders,
of know-no-betters   y neo-Nazis,
of Beowulfs and other   born-again beasts,
of sandaled sombreros   sleeping under cacti,
of Machiavellian   mentes y mouths
of anthropological   autoethnography,
of pretend pachucas   peeling their layers,
of preachers and poets   with puckered lips
of the misused multi-   cultural machinery,
of the Hispanic hodgepodge   hiding their indio,
of the Quetzalcoatls   concealing their conqueror
de la migra meando   marking its turf.

Here, the hemistiched   hemispheres blend,
a vacuum of voices   absorbed in the velvet
paintings of slick   y sexy santos,
of the Aztec icon   at the altar of Aztlán
tripping and turning   transvestite warrior,
of the cyber-cholo   stripping down—¡Simón!
The vato loco's liquid   eye lures us
over borders, their blurred   tumbling barriers,
calling us to come   stare into the cage—
jaula de joda   aquí juntándonos—
the table turned   and tacked to the wall,
lit with votives   licking our luscious
breakfast bowl   of cucarachas on their backs
squirming to free   their feet and fly.

Al mestizaje

In mi gente's hips, la clave
and from mi gente's lips, sale
a fluid, funky lingo fusion
that fools among you call intrusion,
but purity is an illusion.
So if you can't dig la mezcla, ¡chale!

Es indio, africana, gitana, americano,
europeo con nada feo y todo vale:
El papalote, el aguacate, el tecolote, el cacahuete,
y las rucas en sus trocas parqueando con los chucos.
Es que muchas palabras tienen alas.
Son los brazos en abrazos
y el gas en tus chingazos
que siempre nos hacen bailar.
Es el ¿qué? en nuestro choque,
el ¡olé! en mi pozole
que todos van a celebrar.

Hay un oso en sabroso
y tanto ajo en ¡carajo!
que la verdad requiere ver,
y no podemos hacer nada sin un ser.
En la mente de mi gente que es tan inteligente,
hermanos se levantan las manos
y todos los derechos están hechos.
¡Échale! Es como anda la banda. ¡Échale!

Watcha! Mi Totacha te da catos, un mitote de caló.
Es la lengua de mis cuates, un cuetazo chicano.
We call Allah with ¡ojalá!
and send Dios with adiós,
and the alma in tamal feeds us all. ¡Órale!

Cartoon Coyote Goes Po-Mo

Coyote, he never learned the high concept.
He's still rapping at rave parties,
Skateboarding under deconstruction,
past computer networks
(keeps his Olivetti electric in the closet).
Everyone wonders when he'll catch up
like his sister, the computer hacking CEO
of a major pharmaceutical company.
Baby, hers are smart drugs—
performance art provocateurs
tricking the tricksters,
not the white heat Coyote shoots, snorts, swallows.
Hey honey, I can fly
through Ginsberg's naked streets at dawn.
Coyote, he don't quite get it,
applies queer theory to his reading
of Burroughs riding freight train.
In a post-structuralist world
you ride on top of the axles
underneath either end of a boxcar
and watch the sparks fly!
Don't get a cinder in your eye.
That's the cyberpunk way to get
your mojado butt from the frontera
to the fields or the service sweatshops.
Only if coyote don't find you first,
and if he does, he'll eat you alive,
crunch you down like chicharrón
because he don't want no
vegan dietary restrictions;
no one gonna lay that trip on him.
He'd rather gorge himself on your sweet meat
until he autodeconstructs,

blows himself to bits
all up and down the Rio Grande.
And in the time it takes you to find
his plastic voodoo in your Lucky Charms,
he'll be warming a stool in the cantina
at the next border town.
How's that for signification theory?

I am learning
   about the   shattering
   the constant unfolding
of this center within us.

—Valerie Martínez

From the Tongues of Brick and Stone

At Taos, Estevan guides my hands
to the pueblo's clay walls.
I receive their heat, their amber dust.
He recalls his grandmother
teaching him to slide
his palms across the adobe,
so he would remember
the texture of their stories.
So you will know, he says.

All day, I listen to stones—
Camel rock, lava rock,
las montañas Sandía, Jemez, y Sangre de Cristo,
a lump in the holy dirt I draw
from the well at Chimayó,
headstones strung with red and yellow petals
behind la iglesia San Gerónimo
where indios and mexicanos revolted,
took refuge and huddled together
against yet another U.S. invasion.
Inside adobe, they listened
to one another's last breaths.

All night beneath stout beams
in a tiny room of candlelight,
I listen to the ocean of wind
that washes the Santa Fe hills,
its Anasazi tongue as comforting
and unforgiving as Ojo Caliente—
the hot springs with their eyes wise
to what weakens, what replenishes.

Estevan, who is learning to swim,
knows it's a tricky balance
to let go, rest in the hands of others,
trust our own breath
to keep our bodies buoyant,
our faces floating like blossoms
on a pillow of water.

Back in Chicago, I listen above
the horns and wounded mufflers,
the sirens and shrill faces,
the swish and whistle of highways,
above the shudder of the 'L' train,
the clang and clatter of factories,
the boom in the bass that rattles the whole block,
above the noise that calls itself news.

Each winter, I listen to stones
along Lake Michigan, to voices
never removed, who wrap
Pontiac's Rebellion in Algonquian syllables
sent on the skin of the wind. Its chill
still surprises the hollows
between my ribs, then settles
beneath my bones like the arctic
quilt of snow to which I surrender,
arms swishing against the frozen ground
to form an eagle's wings,
flushed cheeks floating on a white cloud.

Here, I press my palms to limestone
and wonder what I will remember.

The Story He Never Told

At this hour, what is dead is restless
and what is living is burning.
—Li-Young Lee

I (1980, United States)

Sí, niña, the night I burned, you dreamed of fire racing through
empty slum streets, engulfing tenements and vacant factories,
razing the roofless condemned to the ground. I know you woke
coughing imagined smoke and shot from your bed to the window
for air, your body fevered with the heat swallowing my twisted car.

And wasn't it fitting that I should burn? I spent my days in the
friction between wife and mistress, booze loosening my tongue
to sear them both. The family should have despised me for the
disgrace, but instead they grew cumbrous in their stumbling
bones as they placed my scorched remains in the cool metal box
and sunk me below the surface.

Oye niña, if it hadn't been for the accident, I would have burned
in some other trap—an elevator, the 18th floor, my own damn bar.
Those flames began to form before you were born, m'ija, twenty-
five years before I was pinned under that web of blistering metal.

II (1951, Korea)

The bitter air stuffs the mountains into my lungs. Afraid to
move, I can only seek shelter behind a wall of pine. Rain flickers
through the web of maple and elm shining like the dark eyes of
my compadre. Wide open, he sucks in the wince of the bayonet
that cleanly sliced his breath. He is slipping into the dark eyes
of the enemy curved almond as those etched in stone effigies of
my own ancestors.

Some time before Cortés and Christ, might the ancient Purépecha
have crossed these Korean mountains? Were they offered rice in
the narrow plains, or did they steal plumes and precious stones?
Force this land's natives to their knees, or bow their own dark
faces to kings' feet? Is it absurd to think they ever met, or might
they have loved once?

The leaves part. I grip my gun tighter, my compadre's neck
cradled in the crook of my free arm. A trigger cocks. I jump,
swing my barrel up. Bullets crack, and both men are falling.

III

It could take days for rescue. My fingernails caked with dirt, I
paw at the cold ground while the bodies wait for their return.
Comrade, enemy—either the dead are brothers or nothing is
human, just a burden on the back of a tired burro. I scrape at the
hole with the snout of my M-1, knowing I should leave them for
the zopilotes and search for my platoon. But how do you leave a
brother's body without so much as a blanket of earth?

Somehow, I tear a grave into the hill just as I have carved my
way through the stomach of this war. And like Huitzilopochtli,
I will emerge decapitating anything that blocks my path—
commie, comrade, patron saint. I look up into the tangle of naked
branches, praying to hear the blades of a chopper slice through
this silence. But Tonatiuh and Tlaloc have fused their power—the
sky is raining fire, mud and rumble hurling me into the hole. I
will burn here in the grave of the one I murdered and the one I
could not save. Oh, Diosito, the earth is an oven.

IV

GIs pull me from the lattice of blood and mud, charred fragments
of flesh and mortar. I want to bury my dead camaradas. I want to
bury my dead, but they will not let me gather the pieces; they will
not help me collect the scorched shards of bone.

I know, child, I know you dreamed of fire the night I burned
in that wreck. But it has all been one long night, Korea's fires
trapping me underneath, always underneath, a heavy and
intricate mesh.

The History Beneath Our Skin

I press the heels of my palms, lean all my weight
into your muscle coiled from neck to waist.

A spring that wound around its prey and snuck
beneath taut skin to breed, this clutching snake.

What memory does it pinch, which lies tangle?
What grief is struck in the rainstorm of its tail?

Is it the cannery heat—thick, sour and damp;
Is it your father's fingers, bent and cramped?

Is it the dust that skims the vines of grapes,
constricting lungs and cutting breath's escape?

Is it the heavy hoist, machete's stoop,
the hiss that skirts your ankles, fills your steps?

Is it your mother's burdens piled and packed,
crossing both countries lashed tight to your back?

Which layers might you shed, which seeds of shame?
Which nightmares nest between your shoulder blades?

If I unsnarl the branches, loosen knots,
will you reveal their weavers, speak their names?

And if my kiss of hands opens your heart,
what poisoned hatchling will slide from my throat?

Centripetal Motion

I have heard the dark hearts
of the stones
that beat once in a lifetime.
—William Pitt Root

So, m'ijo, you want to leave San Bartolo Coyotepec.
You want to try your luck in the big city,
maybe cross to el norte, where everyone is rich.
You want to leave behind these dusty roads,
our casita of thatch and brick,
the goats to milk, hens to feed,
the pollitos crisscrossing over your feet
as you stir black clay para tu papá.

So you want to become el pollito yourself
chirping for a sprinkle of grain,
following coyote's delusive trail
(a tuft of fur, the scent of piss,
chicken scratches and paw prints).
You better develop a sixth sense, m'ijo,
learn to see from every direction.
Coyote traps moonbeams in a steel cage,
weights it with the gnawed bones of many meals
and sends all the light to the bottom of the big river
so no one but the bone pickers will see him cross.
Yet whose sinew is his fill, m'ijo, whose bones his anchors?
Sometimes even God is amused by his tricks.

So you are tired of the curbside puesto,
of hawking the jarras, bowls, whistles and tazas
I have spun from the moistened black dust
de sangre zapoteca y tierra mixteca.
La culpa no es tuya, m'ijo; I cannot blame you

for dreaming of paved streets and tiled floors,
to once eat a meal whose blood has not dried
      under your fingernails.

Sí, en la madrugada te puedes ir. Que te vayas con Dios.
But now, in this afternoon's yellow light,
come sit,   curve your feet around the disk
beneath the shallow cupped stone
      and spin   spin the stone, m'ijo,
feel the weight of Oaxacan black earth
      fall upon the center of motion,
dip your hands into water, slip them to the unshaped clay.

Become blind, m'ijo,   close your hungry eyes and trace
the hollows you will fill,   finger the edge of air.
Spin the stone faster   resist gravity   lift up, up.
      Feel the energy passing from flesh
      to the thousand-year-old field
where I first gathered the black barro of Oaxaca,
where a boy lifted the space
      that spilled into ledges,
pressed soft caves and whirled
      balance into the blooming vessel,
my five-year-old hands placed over my mother's
      and her mother's   and hers   and hers.

Spin with me this jarra, m'ijo, and then you may go
north past the gray riverbank of clay,
through the forests once filled with quetzal flight,
over the Oaxacan hills hewn of red, white, green stone.
      Pero no te olvides, m'ijo,
      to kneel before the dead at Monte Albán.
Pray. Burn copal in this shallow black bowl. Listen.
Someday their ghosts will lead you back
from the land of milk and honey.

Through Arms and Hands

I
Young hands manipulate
brushes like marionettes
        in a whirl. They bend
            the retina's mirror
        into the world beat
of a street mural:

One lifts a sister's fist,
a brother's clanking wrists
        beneath a red moon—
cracked disk spinning into shadow,
the static of her profile
        ripping a predictable skip
through the fleshy folds of sky.

One squints at light falling
        between floorboards.
Under their creaking
        she hides, peeking
at the treaded soles who would sink
        tracks above the bridge
of her brow, crush the bones
        beneath her eyes, fine
as the fiberglass in a fish back.

One turns back
to the hills, dragging his limp leg
        through the dust like a satchel
        of citrus plucked

from the land that sprouts
barbed trees between its wire knees,
        and shakes pellets from its shoes.

One's got the soul for blues,
a jazz jones, reggae rhythm,
syllabic hip hop, bebop,
a mambo, samba, bomba y rhumba,
cumbia con clave de salsa,
        scat a phat rap back, tap tickety-tack,
        wail back a throaty Delta blues
        that rode the rails to the relief
        mosaic of Chicago skyline,

guitar strings picking the glint
        of bottle caps and green glass,
shards of brass blowing
up fire escapes
                down tenement reverberation
rippling off the rim of the hoop,
        his life chalked into tar,
summer steam bubbling up.
        Rebellion tags in cryptic glyph,
        riffs, but never bites
        another's arc of mist.

II
They raise no man's flag.

III
A screech unfurls
        from raven's open beak
        pointed like rage
                into the split sky.

60

The raven-haired women sew
bullets into blouses,
     grind smoke into stone,
         sing the comal's hiss
         as they roll us out on the metate
like a sheet of masa.

Prayer curls around the red nest
     in our chests
like a rattler warming eggs,
     then stretches, unspined,
         a camouflaged line slashing
             into the green-gold blades.

Revolution is a blade
cleaned by the tongue of God.

Diffraction

Rustle of wings   sticks   rain—

     shallow music in cupped hands,

          salmon lapping brambles of water

          as prayer grinds its teeth

     through the breathless slap of birth.

     There is a light at the center of silence.

It bares the mind's deafening riot—

     a jungle gym shaking children's faces,

     noses like polka dots flying

          to concrete,

          spiked hair, feet—

          the heartbeat's omen.

Sirens open like lost mouths

     asleep on broken glass.

At the Base of the Blues Tree:
Una Ofrenda for Jimmy Davis, Chicago Blues Man

(after the painting *Árbol de Blues* by Roberto Valadez)

The hands of this telling tree pull
    him from the cobalt bowl of sky,
bring Jimmy back to the ruins
    of Maxwell Street hunched in dusk.
He stood where strings intersected
    frets like tracks meeting ties
on the Illinois Central's passage
    from the Mississippi Delta,
then followed the bread crumbs
    of troubadours to this steel city.
Twelve-hour shifts beckoned
    mexicanos north on the Union Pacific
from Piedras Negras
    to Pilsen, Back of the Yards.

How many grandparents, mothers and fathers,
    pounded stake into soil,
snuck or were shoved into boxcars,
    leapt onto the train's iron rungs
as it shuddered along the rails
    to foundries where they poured
molten metal, faced hot licks
    of the blast furnace's growl and hiss?
How many lugged themselves north
    to slaughterhouses that drooled
rank puddles at their feet? This,
    so sons and daughters might step off
into another era, choose instruments of wood and metal,
    axes of their own timbre.

This so Jimmy might mix his own palette—
        tune each turquoise pitch and purple tone
into an electric blues old as corridos,
        but new to the mexicanos who came each
Sunday to the market at Maxwell.

New to the ears of Roberto, a boy, who would keep
        his ranchera rhythms close
as a pair of old jeans but grow
        into the blues as he listened
to the heirs of Papa Jackson—
        Johnny Young, Howlin' Wolf, Nighthawk
and Maxwell Jimmy. Now Roberto sits in overalls
        at an easel, splits
the hairs of his brush over how to compose
        this ofrenda, this homage. How
to take Jimmy back in time to the market
        whose merchants once hustled
with tricks for trade ancient as Africa, as Toltec Mexico,
        Maxwell, whose live blues bands
and car radios belting norteño mixes made
        every Sunday a session.

How to take Jimmy back
        to Maxwell's gathering spot where he guzzles
from an aluminum garden blooming atop his amp,
        swings his ax—
fingers climbing its trunk, plucking twigs—
        while our feet tap the roots
of this wailing tree. Notes skip through alleys
        of his voice like gravel
pinging off windshields, lift a pitch
        high enough to singe the autumn sky—
cousin to the red and green gritos of the barrio

only blocks away. Twelve bars spin
like metal rims, stack like hubcaps,
        chords crackling in the tin barrels of his laughter.
When people gather, he sputters,
        What did the one-eyed woman say?
and waits for them to peer into the devil's draw
of his eyes before he roars,
        Where is my one-eyed man?

But we barely get to the punch line, to the end
        of a set, before the mayor swings his ax,
a claw that rips this árbol de blues up by its roots;
        before Chicago swings its wrecking ball
to level homes, stores, restaurants, bars;
        before troops graffiti-blast, scrub and cinch-sack it
all, but one empty wall
        where someone has scrawled Jimmy's name
among the others in this hall of fame:
        Willie, Hound Dog, Honey Boy, Sal,
the many legends who've shared the marrow
        of their music, of Santana's hearty
soup with the bones still in it steaming with sabor,
        and sometimes weeping.

Blues Mama

Gimme a Pig's Foot and a Bottle of Beer
bellows my mama
as she drifts about the house,
dancing with her dust mop,
wailing with her records—
Bessie and Billie, Louie and Duke,
B. B. and Nat King Cole,
The Count and Ray Charles.
I wait for each record to drop,
for Mama's voice to climb
into its grooves,
duet with Sarah Vaughn or Cleo Laine,
Mama's notes strong
and belonging on a black disk.

But instead of cutting LPs,
she cooks, sweeps, scrubs,
and is still singing
"Happiness Is Just a Thing Called Joe"
years after Joe left her alone
with the kids and *some* of the records.

On Saturday nights, after she wakes
from her Valium dreams
of dirty laundry and dust,
Mama escapes, sometimes takes me
with her, to The Clock piano bar.
When we stroll in, Claude winks,
beams a smile wide as his keyboard,
and plunks the first few bars of "Born to Lose,"
a tune he knows Mama has sung
ever since Happy Joe split.

Mama swivels her stool around
to face me, sighs at the ice swirling
around the bottom of her glass,
and says, "You know, honey,
at forty years old, I can't think
of any job I'd like to do, nothing
except be Cleo Laine's personal confidant."

Then she closes her brown, blues-filled eyes
and slams a few for the courage
to reach those low reckless notes
with Claude at The Clock
in the middle of the night:

> *Oh the good life full of fun*
> *seems to be the ideal.*
> *Yes the good life lets you hide*
> *all the sadness you feel . . .*

And I listen to my mama and know
that somehow the music will make home
forever home, no matter how bleak,
no matter how long we are gone.
The music slips underneath our sleep,
etches grooves into our dreams,
and nothing else ever stays
so close for so long.

Song

You shout my name
from beyond my dreams,
beyond the picture window
of this Rosarito beach house.
Rushing from bed to shore
I glimpse their backs—
volcanoes rising out of the sea.
Your back, a blue-black silhouette,
feet wet with the wash of morning waves.
Fountains spring from mammal minds,
my hands lifting a splash of sand.
I'm on my knees,
toes finding a cool prayer
beneath them, fingers pressing
sea foam to my temples,
while you open arms wide as a generation,
raise them to a compass point,
dive.
If you could reach them,
you would ride their fins
under the horizon,
then surf the crash of waves
left in their wake.
And if I could grasp
my own fear,
I'd drown it,
leave it breathless and blue
as this ocean,
as the brilliant backs
of whales
surfacing
for air.

thus it comes
flown, thus it comes
back and home,
for a heartbeat, for a millennium,
to pause

—Paul Celan

Feast

Through her kitchen window
a mother from the south
side of the tracks watches
her little girl twirl, plop
in the garden, dig up
seeds, worms, handfuls of mud

to spread on her pants, cheeks
hair like a warrior
preparing for battle.
Meanwhile, a mother from
the north side releases
her daughter from tea, pats

her beribboned head out
the door. Ruthy skips, lifts
her lacy frills across
the line to her smudged pal.
Double-jointed Dee Dee
shows off, crossing skull-bone

ankles behind her ears.
Unimpressed, Ruthy points
at petals, vines, carrots'
leafy crowns 'til Dee Dee
yanks one sunken gem like
a gold tooth from the ground.

Ruthy frowns at the clumps
clinging to its soiled skin,
so Dee Dee spits on it,

and like a jeweler cleans
a ring, buffs its surface
with her sleeve, polishes

its ridges on her knee.
Clenching its parsley-haired
head, she offers Ruthy
the first crunch, a tongue full
of pungent earth, the salt
of her own sustenance.

When We Moved Away from Tía Elia's and Uncle Karel's, 1968

I almost stayed put.
We lived above them, see,
the minute the door creaked open,
me shouting from the top stair,
"Uncle Kakoo, come get me!"

Tía Elia told me stories day and night,
taught me to draw, paint, write.
I wouldn't climb home
until my eyes had grown
heavy as the whole planet.
She put magic spice in the food,
made it taste like what people
must eat in heaven
or Mexico. She'd sing,
Sana sana, colita de rana
all over my bumps and bruises,
and, believe me, they would disappear.

Uncle Karel always wanted me
to teach him to spell
knight, knife, all those silent-letter words,
'cause he escaped from Yugoslavia
when he turned fourteen
and was still learning English.
He learned Spanish pretty well,
Abuelito's kind that calls owls
tecolotes and straws popotes.
Tía Elia's phone conversations
with Tía Chole never got past him.

He taught me to say English in German:
I vant to go to verk.
Then we tried to add Spanish
but wound up sounding
like Hansel and Gretel in a taquería.
They named me
Cacahuete-Mantequilla-Princess-Red-Cheeks.
And I was the queen of peanut butter
sticking to them
like a sandwich to the roof
of your mouth.

Lecciones de lengua

She is proud of her papá
because he comes
to their little grey school,
converted from army barracks,
to teach español
to Mrs. Benda's fifth grade.
And that means they don't
have to listen to that awful
Señora Beister on TV
with her screech owl version
of "Las mañanitas" and her annoying
forefinger to the ear,
    Escuchen
and then to the lips,
    y repitan.

He teaches them to order
Coca-Cola en el restaurán—
    Señor, quisiera una Coca, por favor—
and the names of all the utensils—
    cuchara, cuchillo, tenedor.
The children look at him funny
when he picks up the knife.
Next week he will demonstrate
the bullfights he watched
in Mexico when he was muy chiquitito.
He will choose a boy to snort, stomp,
charge the red cloth
that Papá will snap
at his side as he dodges

the sharp-horned strike,
stabs invisible swords
into the boy's hide

     and makes the children laugh.

By the Skin of Your Breath

(for Danny)

When you gasped for help and for bits of attic
air, your clogged lungs searching for breath like hands grasped
railings, walls, Mom's arms in the tunnel-blind night,
none of us heard you,

none except our brother, who woke at near-death's
wheeze and blue lips, woke to his own animal
screech and fists, feet slamming the floor in terror,
"Mama, he can't breathe!

Danny can't breathe!" Locked to your frightened gaze, he
couldn't leave you, flee down the stairs to wake us
up, but pleas descended through open air ducts,
flashes of sudden

summer hail that pummeled our ceiling-covered
dreams. I heard Dad rumble from bed to car, Mom
whisk you out the door, as they rushed your flooded
lungs to emergent

hands of doctors. Steve and I hardly breathed then
waiting hours for you to return, a plastic
band around your wrist, but they came without you,
told us you had to

stay for weeks, live under an oxygen tent—
eat there, sleep there, stuck like a lone toy soldier,
homesick, sinking quick in this marshy battle.
Later that week you

     snuck beneath the bed where they found you AWOL—
dauntless rebel, tough as a renegade—air
gliding smoothly into expanding lungs, and
Brother, you came home.

Me and My Cuz

Mother, Father / there's no passing the cup.
I'm going to be a troublemaker / when I grow up.
—Demetria Martínez

Me and my cuz,
the toughest chicks on the south-side strip,
we roar up and down the avenue
in her brother's midnight-blue Barracuda,
with the tiny paint flecks that flicker in the sun,
chrome sparkling and Santana blaring from the Bose,
Dylan embroidered into the seatbelts
with rainbow floss—*Tangled Up in Blue.*

Me and my cuz,
we hang in the park all afternoon,
strut past boys with our long manes flowing,
our faded jeans snug and patched
to match our hips' swing to the right and left.
We dare them to call us over for a little cervecita.

Me and my cuz,
we cruise past Tío's bar on Saturday afternoons
to perch on the spinning stools
and sip soda while he washes glasses
and mops the sticky floors.

His voice deepens when he begins
Lesson Número Uno:
"Pretty soon you girls will be old enough
to come into taverns like this,
y escúchame bien,

don't you ever let me catch you
take your change off the bar.
Snap up your dollar bills,
pero dejen las monedas.
We bartenders got to make a living too."

Then he instructs us on backdoor escapes
from slimy pendejos
and fifty ways to leave los cabrones
"who just sit on these stools every night
guzzling Budweiser and waiting
patiently to pay you pretty little compliments
that turn into babies y chingazos,
pots, pans y muchas lágrimas."

Me and my cuz
we got it down, Lesson Número Uno:
bars, boys and blue Barracudas
for the rest of our lives.

Hay una mujer / There Is a Woman

And there is a woman coming out of her mouth.
Hay una mujer saliendo de la boca.
—Cherríe Moraga

Hay una mujer
in the chile's spit
una mujer in the seed
between your teeth
in the molcajete pulp
of our disturbed sleep
in the grind
of his tired break-
fast thrust out the door

Always there is a woman
who will not click in
to the tintintín
of heels tempting her
with tricks
in the concrete night

Hay una mujer
in your jungle of hair
combing feathers
to the floor
A woman weaving them
into her danza

Una mujer piercing
the fish of her river
pescando pescando
A woman who feeds

them to the bear
in the cave of our fear

We cannot see her
pero hay una mujer
in the vowel
at the back
of your throat
where she swims
along the fins
of your consonants
the tails
of your slippery words

Hay una mujer Hay una mujer
Hay mujer Hay mujer
¡Ay mujer! ¡Ay ay ay ay ay mujer!
I mujer! I mujer!
Don't you be eyein' that mujer
Don't you be eyein' her now

There is a woman
in the snow underfoot
raining hail
on your uncapped head

Hay una mujer
spinning water into webs
She's a spider
a woman yelping with the pack
Coyote's been known
to grow breasts
when it suits her/him/her

Hay una mujer
de México
una de Yemen
a woman from the swell
of Lake Michigan

Hay una mujer
scaling rocks in Ecuador
paddling down the Nile
holding onto her hammock
in the San Blas wind
whispering Malay in a rainforest
swinging from sky-
scrapers in Japan

Hay una mujer de Europa
riding a train to Belfast
de Ohio hitchin' to New York
Una mujer flippin' you
for inchin' in her lane
yellin' ¡Chíngate cabrón!

There's a woman
in the backseat
a woman in the cockpit
a woman planing grass
in the Everglades

Hay una mujer
del barrio en Califas
una mujer del barrio en Chicago
una del barrio en Denver
en El Paso en Miami
en tu backyard

There is a woman dead
one hundred years
in the fields
Una cantando
singing herself to sleep

Hay una mujer in the PLO
the CIA IRS IRA
in AIM
a woman aiming
at your soft spot

Siempre hay una mujer
who wants out
a woman who flees
and a woman who waits

in her pinstriped best
in her zoot suit
a woman wearing
your white collar to bed
crumpling it
messing with ya

There is la mujer you suckle
the woman you cling to
la mujer you cry for
the woman you sing to
la mujer you work for
the woman you double-cross
la mujer who always knows
the woman who tongues
the questioning curve
of your ear in a dream
that repeats for the rest of your life

She's racing semis
'round an oval track
She's riding broncs bareback
She's hustling
in the subway
of your sin
nickel for a prayer
dime for a sign

She's rumbling in the railways
of your brain
stumbling 'long the tracks
in your lost shoes

She's slipping eggs
into his sperm
impregnating a hundred
little hims
and coaching
all his labors

Hay una mujer
braiding the fibers
of your *yes* and *no*
tying slipknots
en tu estómago
Una mujer at the congas
in your chest
sending sparks
down your neck

Una mujer whooshing
up through the arches
of your feet and out
your fingertips

whitewater woman   *red earth woman*   *yellow river woman*
in you   *in you*   *in you*
woman in you   *woman in you*   *woman in you*
woman in you   *woman in you*   *woman in you*

mujer de arena   *black sea woman*
en ti   *in you*
arena en ti   *woman in you*
arena en ti   *woman in you*

black sea woman in you
whitewater woman in you
red earth woman in you
yellow river woman in you
la arena en ti en ti en ti

You want what you want
and you want her
a woman who can
stir you but not spin
your head around
a woman who
can't hit high tide
can't run your banks
shoot your falls
surf your wake
a woman who
can't fly without you

Pero siempre
always
hay una mujer
there is a woman
who can

Shift

when summer debris   tangles

                   like shed

                        skin   around fingers

and feet   of drift-

                                    wood

sculpted goddesses   abandoned

                 in sand

        grip the ground with splintered

                            hands

gravity funnels

          the hungry arches   of knuckles   sliding

     into palms   and wrists

back away

        the earth forming   tiny aqueducts

              between   bones   of toes

       for coming rivulets   of rain

by autumn   eyes spill

              into each other

    thighs fall   chest caves

fewer arrows of sun

                but the belly   still   rises

                        a small hill turned

                        on its side   to meet

                              the ice

                its last warmth   seeping

   like rays of

          blistered headlights

                    the only car on the highway

before dawn

Zacuanpapalotls

(in memory of José Antonio Burciaga, 1947–1996)

We are chameleons. We become chameleon.
—José Antonio Burciaga

We are space between—
the black-orange blur
of a million Monarchs
on their two-generation migration
south to fir-crowned Michoacán
where tree trunks will sprout feathers,
a forest of paper-thin wings.

Our Mexica cocooned
in the membranes de la Madre Tierra
say we are reborn zacuanpapalotls,
mariposas negras y anaranjadas
in whose sweep the dead whisper.

We are between—
the flicker of a chameleon's tail
that turns his desert-blue backbone
to jade or pink sand,
the snake-skinned fraternal twins
of solstice and equinox.

The ashen dawn, silvering dusk,
la oración as it leaves the lips,
the tug from sleep,
the glide into dreams
that husk our mestizo memory.

We are—
one life passing through the prism
of all others, gathering color and song,
cempazuchil and drum
to leave a rhythm scattered on the wind,
dust tinting the tips of fingers
as we slip into our new light.

Glossary

This glossary contains only those Spanish words and phrases not found in standard Spanish dictionaries or whose meaning differs from that found in such dictionaries. Also included are Mexica (Aztec) and Maya words and other names that may be unfamiliar to the reader. Words and phrases are listed by poem, in order of appearance.

"Empty Spaces" (p. 3)
i griegas y erres   the letters *y* and double *r* in the Spanish alphabet

"Turning" (pp. 15–18)
La Villita   a neighborhood in Chicago
los tzotziles   the Tzotzil Mayans

"Our Language" (pp. 32–33)
hache   the letter *h* in the Spanish alphabet

"Sound Waves: Intensidad—Ñ" (pp. 37–38)
Kukulkan   Mayan name for Quetzalcoatl, the plumed serpent god of Mexica (Aztec) mythology

"Report from the Temple of Confessions in Old Chicano English" (pp. 44–45)
pachucas   Chicana homegirls of the 1940s

Quetzalcoatl the Mexica plumed serpent god
la migra the border patrol
Aztlán the mythical homeland of the Mexica people in what is
 now the southwestern United States
cholo Chicano homeboy of the 1960s and 70s
¡Simón! Yes! (slang)
vato loco crazy dude

"The Story He Never Told" (pp. 53-55)
Purépecha Mexican indigenous tribe often referred to as
 Tarascans
Huitzilopochtli the Hummingbird Wizard, Mexica god of war
Tlaloc the Mexica god of rain and fertility
Tonatiuh the Mexica sun god who rules the fifth or current age

"Through Arms and Hands" (pp. 59-61)
masa cornmeal dough, which is spread in cornhusks to make
 tamales

"At the Base of the Blues Tree" (pp. 63-65)
corridos popular Mexican narrative ballads
norteño a kind of Mexican *ranchera* song from northern
 Mexico

"Hay una mujer / There Is a Woman" (pp. 81-86)
Califas California

"Zacuanpapalotls" (pp. 89-90)
zacuanpapalotls Monarch butterflies
cempazuchil marigold